ISRAEL
the people

Debbie Smith

A Bobbie Kalman Book

The Lands, Peoples, and Cultures Series

 Crabtree Publishing Company
www.crabtreebooks.com

The Lands, Peoples, and Cultures Series

Created by Bobbie Kalman

Coordinating editor
Ellen Rodger
Proofreader: Adrianna Morganelli

Consulting editor
Virginia Mainprize

Project development, writing, editing, and design
First Folio Resource Group, Inc.
Pauline Beggs
Tom Dart
Marlene Elliott
Kathryn Lane
Debbie Smith

Revisions and updates
Plan B Book Packagers
Redbud Editorial

Special thanks to
Steven G. Esrati; Shawky J. Fahel, J. G. Group of Companies; David H. Goldberg, Ph.D., Canada-Israel Committee; Steven Katari; Taali Lester, Israel Government Tourist Office; Alisa Siegel and Irit Waidergorn, Consulate General of Israel; and Khaleel Mohammed

Photographs
Steven Allan: p. 5 (top), p. 15 (both), p. 16 (bottom), p. 20 (top), p. 24 (left), p. 28; Sammy Avnisan/Photo Researchers: p. 16 (top); Pavel Bernshtam/Shutterstock, Inc.: p. 18; Natalia Bratslavsky/Shutterstock, Inc.: p. 11 (top); Odelia Cohen/Shutterstock, Inc.: p. 24 (right), p. 25 (top); Express Newspapers/Archive Photos: p. 9; Lior Filshteiner/Stutterstock, Inc.: cover; Annie Griffiths Belt/Corbis: p. 22, p. 23 (top); Israel Government Tourist Office: p. 23 (bottom); Jorge Pedro Barradas de Casais/Shutterstock, Inc.: p. 4 (left); Boris Katsman/Shutterstock, Inc.: p. 1, p. 10 ; Nir Levy/Shutterstock, Inc.: p. 11 (bottom), p. 25 (bottom); Arkady Mazor/Shutterstock, Inc.: p. 19 (top); David Mckee/Shutterstock, Inc.: p. 14 ; Richard T. Nowitz: p. 3, p. 11 (middle), p. 12 (bottom), p. 13, p. 19 (bottom), p. 20 (bottom), p. 21, p. 26–27 (all), p. 29–30 (all); Nola Rin/Shutterstock, Inc.: p. 5 (bottom); Howard Sandler/Shutterstock, Inc.: p. 31; Inga Spence/Tom Stack & Associates: p. 17; Josef F. Stuefer/Shutterstock, Inc.: p. 25 (middle); Albert H. Teich/Shutterstock, Inc.: p. 4 (bottom); Khirman Vladimir/Shutterstock, Inc.: p. 12 (top)

Illustrations
William Kimber. The back cover shows an ibex, a wild goat native to Israel. A pair of olive branches, a symbol of peace, appear at the head of each section.

Cover
Boys cool off on a hot summer day by jumping into the ocean from an old brick wall at Akko, Israel.

Title page
Jewish men pray at Jerusalem's Western Wall.

Library and Archives Canada Cataloguing in Publication

Smith, Debbie, 1962 Nov. 17-
    Israel : the people / Debbie Smith.

(Lands, peoples, and cultures series)
Includes index.
ISBN 978-0-7787-9312-0 (bound).--ISBN 978-0-7787-9680-0 (pbk.)

    1. Israel--Social conditions--Juvenile literature. I. Title. II. Series.

HN660.A8S58 2007   j956.94   C2007-906228-8

Library of Congress Cataloging-in-Publication Data

Smith, Debbie, 1962-
    Israel. The people / Debbie Smith.
        p. cm. -- (The lands, peoples, and cultures series)
    "A Bobbie Kalman Book."
    Includes index.
    ISBN-13: 978-0-7787-9312-0 (rlb)
    ISBN-10: 0-7787-9312-5 (rlb)
    ISBN-13: 978-0-7787-9680-0 (pb)
    ISBN-10: 0-7787-9680-9 (pb)
    1. Israel--Social life and customs--Juvenile literature. I. Title. II. Series.

DS112.S65 2007
956.94--dc22   2007041475

Crabtree Publishing Company

www.crabtreebooks.com   1-800-387-7650

Published in Canada
Crabtree Publishing
616 Welland Ave.
St. Catharines, ON
L2M 5V6

Published in the United States
Crabtree Publishing
PMB16A
350 Fifth Ave., Suite 3308
New York, NY 10118

Published in the United Kingdom
Crabtree Publishing
White Cross Mills
High Town, Lancaster
LA1 4XS

Published in Australia
Crabtree Publishing
386 Mt. Alexander Rd.
Ascot Vale (Melbourne)
VIC 3032

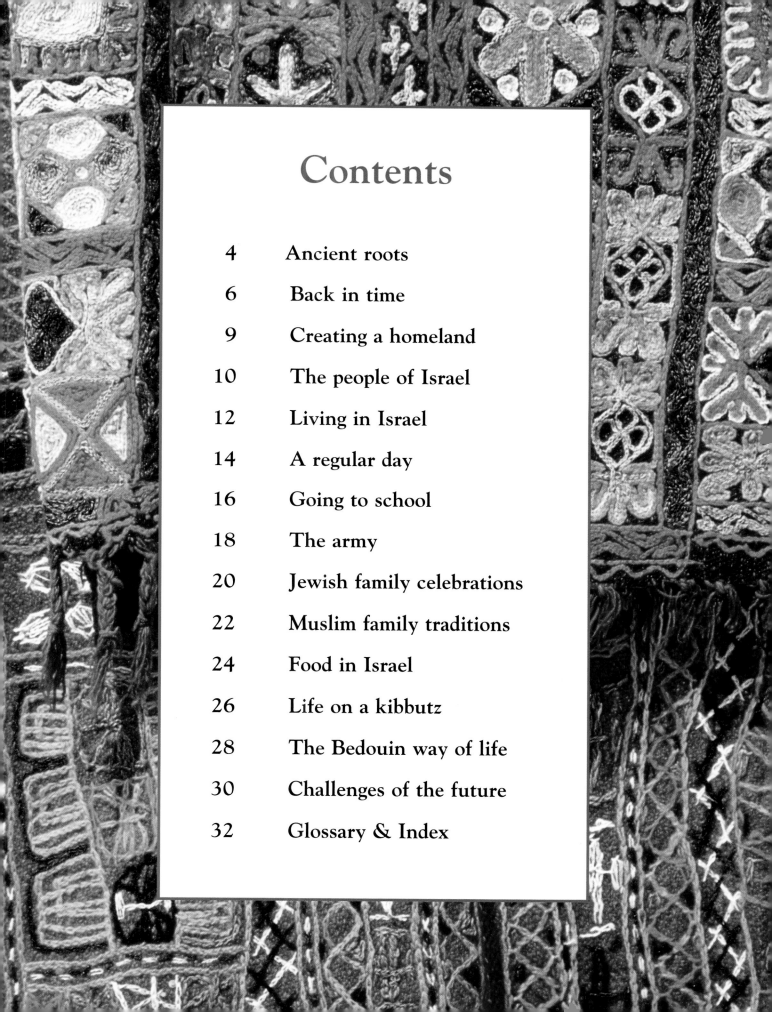

Contents

Israel is a new nation with ancient roots. The State of Israel was founded in 1948, but people have lived on the land for thousands of years. Determined to survive in a harsh **environment**, the people of Israel have created a home where they have prospered.

Israel's population has grown quickly since it became a country in 1948. The Jews and Arabs who lived on the land before that time have been joined by people from around the world. Each group has brought its own culture and **traditions**, adding to Israel's diversity. In spite of differences among the people, they all have one thing in common: they feel a deep attachment to the land.

(below) A young Arab girl wears a scarf with a traditional pattern over her head and shoulders as a sign of respect and modesty.

(above) Old robes, new ways! This Eastern Orthodox Christian priest chats on a cell phone while on a street in Jerusalem.

(left) An elderly Arab takes a rest in the shade. A kaffiyeh is draped over his head and held in place with a black akkal.

(below) This Israeli brother and his sisters share a kiss while on a family trip to the beach.

5

Back in time

The land that we now call Israel has a very long history. Many powerful **empires** marched through the land. Each of them left its mark and changed the lives of the people who lived there.

Jews arrive, led by Abraham

Canaanites 2100 B.C.

Jews flee to Egypt, led by Jacob, Abraham's grandson, to avoid famine.

Jews return escaping slav in Egypt

Philistines 1200 B.C.

Prosperous Judea

Three thousand years ago, King David, the great king of the Jews, waged war over the land of Israel, then known as Canaan. He defeated a people called the Philistines, and renamed the country Judea. King David's son, King Solomon, built a beautiful limestone temple in Jerusalem. It gleamed with beaten gold and polished cedar. Jews from all over Judea traveled to Jerusalem to pray at this great house of worship.

Under King Solomon, the Jews enjoyed peace. Solomon developed copper mines and built new towns, but the people had to pay heavily for his ambitious plans. They began to fight with one another and after Solomon's death they split the Judean Kingdom in two: Israel in the north and Judah in the south.

Judean Kingdom 1020 B.C. - 930 B.C.

Assyrian Rule 720 B.C.

Babylonian Rule 586 B.C.

Babylonians exile Jews

Greek Rule 333 B.C.

Persian Rule
538 B.C.

Persians
allow the Jews
to return

Hasmonean Rule 142 B.C.

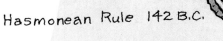

Roman Rule 63 B.C.

Byzantine Rule 313 A.D.

Masada

The Roman Empire was huge and powerful. The Jews did not like their Roman rulers. In 66 A.D., they rose up against the Romans and took over the city of Jerusalem. The Jewish people fought off the Romans for three years. Finally, the Romans stormed Jerusalem, destroyed the temple, and sold many Jews into slavery.

Almost one thousand Jews held out against the Romans, occupying a mountaintop fortress, called Masada, that looked out over the Dead Sea. It took two years for thousands of Roman soldiers to build a ramp up the cliffs and to break through the fortress walls. When they finally succeeded, they discovered that all but seven people were dead. The rest of the Jewish men, women, and children had killed themselves. To them, becoming slaves was a fate worse than death.

Jews scattered
throughout
the Roman
Empire

Diaspora

After another Jewish uprising in 132 A.D., the Romans overpowered the Jewish people. They renamed Judea "Palestine" and scattered most of the Jews throughout the Roman Empire. Some Jews managed to escape to northern Europe and avoid slavery, while a handful of deeply religious Jews remained in and around Jerusalem. This scattering of the Jews around the world is called the **Diaspora**. Even though the Jews were spread throughout Europe, northern Africa, and the Middle East, they managed to keep their religion and communities alive. Jews everywhere continued to pray that one day they would return to their **homeland**.

7

Crusades 1099

Arabs and Crusaders

By the eleventh century, Palestine was ruled by the Arabs. In 1099, a group of European knights launched a series of wars, or Crusades, to claim Jerusalem and the **holy** land of Palestine for the Christian Church. During the First Crusade, all the Muslims and Jews living in Jerusalem were killed. The knights of the Crusades continued to raid Palestine for the next 200 years. The great Arab warrior Saladin forced the Crusaders out of Jerusalem in 1187. The English king Richard the Lion-Heart fought against Saladin to try to regain Jerusalem during the Third Crusade. The battle ended with a **truce**. King Richard withdrew after Saladin agreed to allow Christians to visit the holy places in Jerusalem.

Mamluk Rule 1291

Ottoman Rule 1516

British Rule 1917

Israel 1948

8

Jews return to the homeland

By the late 1800s, most Jews around the world had never lived in the land of Israel. Even so, they thought of it as their true home. Their **ancestors** had left the country centuries ago, believing that one day they would return.

Zionism

During the Diaspora, Jews were **discriminated** against because of their religion. Many began to believe that the only solution to **anti-Semitism** was to create a separate state where all Jews could live together. In the 1890s, the political movement Zionism was born to bring the Jews of the Diaspora together in the land of Israel. In 1917, the British government stated its support for the Zionist cause. Jews, mostly from eastern Europe, began to **immigrate** to Palestine in greater and greater numbers.

The Holocaust

Between 1933 and 1945, in Germany and in much of western and eastern Europe, the Nazis, led by Adolf Hitler, organized the extermination of the Jews. In every country that the Nazis invaded during World War II, they rounded up the Jewish people and put them to death or imprisoned them in concentration camps. The conditions in these camps were horrible, and many of the prisoners who were not ordered to do hard labor were killed. During this period, known as the Holocaust, over six million Jews died.

After a long and uncomfortable journey, Jewish immigrants catch their first glimpse of the port of Haifa in their new home, Israel. They scramble as high as they can up the rigging of the boat to get a better view.

A plan for a new country

After World War II, the need for a Jewish state became more obvious. Hundreds of thousands of Jews were left without a home after the war. In 1947, the Zionist dream came true. The United Nations proposed splitting Palestine in two. One part was meant for the Jewish people. The other part was saved for the Arabs who had lived in Palestine for over 1,000 years. The Jewish people agreed with the plan. The Arab leaders did not.

Israel is here!

On May 14, 1948, the State of Israel declared its independence. The Jews finally had the homeland they had dreamed of. The following day, Israel's Arab neighbors invaded. The War of Independence had begun. After fifteen months, Israel was victorious. The Jewish people still had their homeland, but the land that was meant for the Arabs of Palestine was now divided between Israel's Arab neighbors.

Many different groups of people now live in Israel. Over 76 percent of the population are Jewish, 16 percent are Arab, and about 2 percent are Christian. The Druze and other smaller communities make up the rest.

Come to Israel!

Judaism is both a religion and a culture. Jews believe in one God and follow the teachings of their holy book, the Torah. Before Israel was declared a state in 1948, Jews were a **minority** in the land. After Independence, a huge wave of Jewish immigrants settled in the country. In just five years, Israel's Jewish population doubled. At first, most immigrants came from Europe. Later, Jews from other places, such as Morocco, Ethiopia, and Russia, immigrated to Israel. Today, Jews from all over the world continue to arrive on Israel's doorstep every day. Even though all these people share the same religion, their cultures are very different. They eat different foods and speak the languages of the countries they come from.

Operation airlift

Entire communities of Jews were brought to Israel by airplane. Operation Magic Carpet moved 45,000 Jews from Yemen in 1949, and Operation Ali Baba transported 123,000 Jews from Iraq in 1950. During Operation Solomon in 1991, approximately 14,000 Ethiopian Jews, escaping war and **famine**, arrived in Israel in a single day!

Arabs

Arabs are the largest minority in Israel. They speak Arabic, one of the two official languages of Israel. Most Arabs are Muslims. They are followers of the religion of Islam. They believe in one God, Allah, and his **prophet**, Muhammad. Other Arabs are Christians. They follow the teachings of Jesus Christ. Arabs lived in the country before 1948, when it was called Palestine. For that reason, many Arabs in Israel today still call themselves Palestinians.

Jews make up over 76 percent of Israel's population. Israel is their homeland.

Druze

The Druze also speak Arabic. Their religion is based on Islam, but 800 years ago they broke away from traditional Muslim beliefs. Because of this, they were treated poorly. The Druze moved to secluded villages in the mountains where they could live in peace. In Israel, the Druze still live in the mountainous northern regions of the Galilee and the Golan Heights.

Only a few people in each Druze community know the secrets of their religion. They pass on their knowledge to other chosen Druze.

Bedouins

The Bedouin are nomadic Arab tribes that have traditionally moved from place to place in the desert. They move in search of grazing land and water for their herds of sheep, goats, and camels. In Israel, most Bedouin live in the south, in the Negev Desert.

(above) These young Orthodox men are debating religious ideas.

(right) A Druze elder talks about his culture with his grandson.

(left) Many Bedouin live on the edge of modern life, still owning camels but now living in permanent settlements most of the year.

11

Living in Israel

As you travel through Israel, you will see many of the same kinds of homes, buildings, and green spaces as in other parts of the world, but Israeli communities also have certain features that make them unique.

Houses

Houses in Israel are often white with flat roofs. The houses are made of concrete, and the flat roofs makes it easy to build a second floor if more space is needed. Many houses have beautiful walled gardens, where families and friends sit and chat on cool nights.

Apartments

Most Israelis live in cities. Since the big cities are crowded, many families live in apartments rather than houses. Often, a family owns an apartment unit and shares the responsibility of taking care of the building with other tenants. The floors are often tiled to help keep the apartment cool in the hot summer. From an apartment balcony you can look out over the city on a cool evening, and yell to your friends walking below.

(top) This house in Jerusalem has a walled garden.

(left) The sun makes a great water heater in Israel. These apartments in Be'er Sheva have their own solar panels to heat their water in rooftop tanks.

12

Refugee camps

When the War of Independence broke out, some Arab residents of Palestine stayed in the country, while others moved to **refugee** camps in the neighboring Arab countries of Egypt, Jordan, Syria, and Lebanon. Today, hundreds of thousands of Palestinians continue to live in refugee camps. Some of these camps are in the Gaza Strip and in the West Bank, to the west of the Jordan River. These two areas came under Israeli control after the Six Day War in 1967.

Life in refugee camps is extremely difficult. The camps are very basic and crowded. The electricity in many camps is regularly cut off. Many refugees live in simple concrete block housing. The alleyways between the shelters are not paved. During the summer, the camps are dusty and when it rains, the streets turn to mud. Many refugees are unemployed.

*(below) **In her spacious tent, a Bedouin woman flips** **pita** **bread with a quick flick of the wrist.***

Bedouin tents

Traditional Bedouins in the Negev Desert live in goat wool tents that shelter them from the fierce desert wind. The largest piece of cloth is used for the tent's roof. Smaller strips of wool are used for the walls. When it rains and the wool gets wet, the fibers expand and keep the rain out. When the weather is warm, the sides can be rolled up to allow cool breezes to waft through the tent.

The inside of a Bedouin tent is cozy. The ceiling is usually low, but it can be raised or lowered even more with tent poles of different lengths. A fire for cooking burns in the center of the tent. Colorful, handmade rugs and cushions cover parts of the sand floor. A curtain divides the tent in two. One side is for the men and their guests, the other side is for the women. It does not take long for Bedouins to pack up their tents and belongings before moving on to their next site. In just two hours they can leave without a trace.

People from many different countries have brought their ways of life to Israel. Some routines are common throughout Israel, while others reflect the customs of one particular culture.

Afternoon break

All over the world, many people who live in warm climates take a break during the hottest time of day. Israel is no exception. Between 1:00 p.m. and 4:00 p.m. many parts of the country grow a little quieter. Stores close, the streets become emptier, and people have a nap. Some apartment buildings even have a rule that there be no noise during this time.

Haggling as sport

There are modern supermarkets and malls in Israel, but many people still prefer to do their shopping in small stores. In market places and along the narrow streets of old cities, shopkeepers display their goods in stalls. They compete with one another by yelling out the prices of their goods. Prices are usually flexible. The shopkeeper's first price is often the beginning of a long and involved ritual called **haggling**. If you accept the first price, you might even disappoint the shopkeeper because they like to bargain!

Parks are a peaceful place to stop and rest during a busy day.

14

Socializing

The warm weather of Israel is perfect for getting together with friends and family outdoors. People meet in cafés, play backgammon in the shade, and stroll along city streets. Strolling is so popular that it has a special name – *lehizdangeff*. This word comes from the name of one of the busiest streets in Tel Aviv, Dizengoff Street, where people wander leisurely at any time of day or night.

(right) The lush Banias Springs in the Golan Heights are a cool getaway from the city.

A woman weighs fresh greens as her customers try to convince her to give them a special price.

Leisure and sports

Until recently, most Israelis only had one day off a week, and that was Saturday. On that day many businesses were closed and buses did not run. Now, many people also get Friday off. With two days off in a row, people often travel within the country, going on hiking trips or swimming at the beach.

Playing sports is a favorite way of spending free time. Basketball is very popular in Israel. Many schoolyards have a basketball court and apartment buildings have hoops attached to the walls for pick-up games of one-on-one. Israelis are also avid soccer fans. Israel has a national league, as well as a team that competes internationally.

Every four years, the Maccabiah Games are held in Tel Aviv. These Jewish Olympics, as they are often called, bring together Jewish athletes from around the world to compete in a variety of sports.

15

In Israel, everyone between the ages of six and sixteen must go to school, but not everyone goes to the same type of school. There are two types of public schools for Jewish children. One type focuses on religion and one type does not. Arab and Druze children are taught in Arabic in a separate public school system. Finally, there are private schools that are run by various religious groups and other organizations.

Studying culture

In both Arab and Jewish schools, students learn about their history and culture. They also learn math, science, and languages. Many students in Jewish schools take Arabic classes, while students in Arab schools begin to study Hebrew in the third grade. Most students in both Jewish and Arab schools also study English.

If your friend goes to an Arab school and you go to a Jewish school, you might have difficulty spending a day together. Arab school children get Fridays off, while Hebrew schools close on Saturday for *Shabbat*, the Jewish day of rest.

(above) Teenage boys study the Torah at school.

(below) Orthodox Jewish girls play tag.

David's day

"David, Ari, time to get up." David is nine and is in grade five. His brother Ari is seventeen years old. They go to different schools but their mom gets them both up at 6:00 a.m., so they can be ready to start school at 8:00 a.m. "I'm first in the bathroom." Ari gives David's upper bunk a kick, laughs, and heads down the hall. David lies in his bunk and thinks about the day ahead. It is going to be a good day. David will have his first English class.

Ari is in grade twelve. This year he must take an exam called a *bagrut*. The bagrut covers all the material he has ever learned. He cannot go to university without passing it. The school year has only just begun, and Ari is already nervous about the exam. "Your turn," says Ari as he charges back into their shared bedroom. David tumbles out of his top bunk. He has to hurry because his cousin Eli will be by soon. They walk to school together each morning. Eli goes to a religious school near David's school. Eli wears a **kippah** on his head and a prayer shawl under his shirt called a *tallit katan*. Eli hopes to go on to a **yeshiva** high school where he will study Jewish life. Maybe one day he will go to a religious university and become a **rabbi**.

"Hurry, Eli is at the door." David's mom gives him a hug and the boys are out on the street in no time. "Shalom Eli!" David waves as Eli rushes up the steps to his school. David sets off toward his own school. "Shalom David!" yells Irit, the crossing guard who is a few classes ahead of David. "You're late. You're going to miss the bus to Masada." Masada! David had completely forgotten about the special field trip. Now he really has to hurry.

Crossing guards pose together next to a crosswalk. David slipped into the photo as he was rushing to school. Can you spot him?

David hurries across and down the street. David slips into class a few minutes late. Morah Rachel, his teacher, does not seem to notice. She is trying to get the class to settle down. Everyone is very excited about Masada.

"Is everyone ready?" calls Morah Rachel. "We're going to leave for Masada right away since we don't want to walk up the long Snake Path at the hottest time of the day. Did everyone remember to bring a lunch?" Luckily, David's father had packed him a sandwich.

The school trip is great and David learns a lot about the Jews' **rebellion** at Masada. As soon as he gets home to his family's apartment, he grabs a piece of honey cake, then races off to his karate class. His class finishes just in time for dinner at 7:00 p.m. His dad is making David's favorite dish: *shakshouka*, eggs in tomato sauce. David hopes that after dinner the whole family will go for a walk and have coffee and ice cream in a café.

17

The army

Israel's first 60 years have not been peaceful. There have been wars between Israel and its Arab neighbors, and clashes between Jews and Arabs living in the country. For security and safety, Israel has had to maintain a large, well-trained defense force.

Mandatory service

For Jewish and many Druze Israelis, being in the army is a part of growing up. After high school, when they are eighteen years old, they must join the Israel Defense Force (IDF). Druze who are originally from neighboring Arab countries and Israeli Arabs do not join the army. If another war broke out between Israel and one of its Arab neighbors, they might feel that they were attacking their own people.

(above) IDF training includes battle simulations, where soldiers act as if they were in a real battle.

Men usually serve in the army for three years and women serve for two. They live on separate army bases. Food, clothing, shelter, and even some entertainment are provided by the IDF. The soldiers receive only a little pocket money for themselves. Every other weekend, they are allowed to go home. On Saturday, their families can visit the base.

In training

The first day at the army base is exciting and confusing. Everyone is given a new uniform. Long-haired men have their heads shaved, and women who have long hair tie it back. By the end of the day, everyone is wearing green fatigues and combat boots. Everyday the soldiers are awakened at 5:00 a.m. Before breakfast, they do their difficult morning exercises. Training continues all day. Some soldiers attend courses to learn specialized skills, such as tank repair or radar.

Most men train to become combat soldiers. Their physical training is intense. Some may become pilots or join the navy. Other men and women are trained in different fields. For example, they may become mapmakers, computer programmers, or clerks.

What a day!

After a long, hard day the new soldiers collapse into bed. Few Israeli soldiers get more than five hours rest a night. Eventually, they become used to the difficult routine and stay up later, chatting and playing cards with their new friends.

After the army

After serving full-time, soldiers go on to university or find a job. Some may choose to work full-time in the army. The others must join the reserve, where they will train and serve in the army for a few weeks each year. If a war breaks out and more soldiers are needed, the reserves will help defend the country.

(above) **It is not unusual to see a soldier praying at the Western Wall.**

(below) **Soldiers take a break from regular training to compete in a game of tug of war.**

In Israel, as in many other countries, life passages such as birth, **coming of age**, marriage, and death are marked by special observances and celebrations. Jewish families look to the Torah to learn about traditions that play a part in these events.

Birth
Eight days after a Jewish boy is born he is named at a *brit milah*, a ceremony where he officially joins the Jewish community. At this ceremony, he is also **circumcised**. A girl can be named any time after birth. A party is held after the ceremony.

Growing up
When a Jewish boy reaches thirteen years of age, he is considered old enough to participate in religious life. A special ceremony, called a *bar mitzvah*, marks his passage into adulthood. Girls can have a similar ceremony called a *bat mitzvah*. On their special day, they read a passage from the Torah at **synagogue**. Then a party usually follows.

(left) **At his bar mitzvah,** *relatives help a teenager carry a heavy Torah scroll to the holy Western Wall.*

(below) **A teenager prepares for her bat mitzvah.**

Marriage

A Jewish wedding is a time of great celebration. The couple say their vows under a *chuppah*, a canopy that symbolizes their new home. A rabbi pronounces the couple married, and they each take a sip of wine from a glass. To remind the couple that suffering and joy often go hand in hand, the groom steps on the glass, crushing it. Then the party begins with food, dancing, and cries of *"Mazel tov!"* or *"Congratulations!"*

Death

Jewish funerals are held as soon as possible after someone dies. From the time of death to the time of the funeral, a watcher keeps the body company and keeps a memorial candle lit. Specially trained volunteers, known as the *Chevrei Kaddisha*, prepare the body for burial according to Jewish religious law. For the week following the funeral, the immediate family observes a time of mourning called *shiva*. During this time, they say a special prayer called *kaddish*. Friends and relatives visit the mourners to pray with them, to comfort them, and to bring them food. A ceremony is held later in the year when a tombstone is placed at the grave.

(above) **Jewish brides of Yeminite descent wear elaborately embroidered clothes and heavy silver jewelry at their weddings. Yemen is a country in the Arabian peninsula. Here, a bride's relatives help her dress for the ceremony.**

(left) **A rabbi reads aloud from a decorated ketubah, a Jewish marriage certificate.**

21

Muslim family celebrations involve the community and are centered around religion.

Birth

After birth, the first words that a Muslim baby hears are the words of the Shahadah whispered into its right ear: "Allah is the only God and Muhammad is his true Messenger." The family gathers to name the child and all boys are circumcised. At the naming, thanks are given to Allah and food is blessed and served. A newborn baby is a gift from Allah, and large families are considered a blessing.

(below) Schoolgirls wash before mosque.

Growing up

Children start accompanying their parents to the mosque, a place of worship, when they are very young. As they grow older, they are taught how to pray, they memorize parts of their holy book, the Qur'an, and they learn about the principles of Islam. By the time they are twelve or thirteen years old, Muslims are responsible for religious practices, such as fasting during the holy month of Ramadan.

Marriage

Living with an extended family is common among Muslims in Israel. Marriages are not only the joining together of two people, but the joining together of two families. Marriages are sometimes arranged by the families, but if couples do not like the mates that their families have chosen for them, they can refuse.

Muslim marriages are often public celebrations that can last for seven days. Every night before the wedding, separate celebrations are held for family and friends at the homes of both the groom's and the bride's parents. On the day of the wedding, the bride and groom go to the mosque. The bride stands in front of the women, to one side of the *imam* or religious leader. The groom stands on the other side, in front of the men. The couple shares a sweet drink. Then, before a contract is made, the *imam* asks the bride and groom three times if they are willing to get married, just to be sure. A large celebration follows, where sometimes 700 to 900 people gather for music, dancing, and a feast.

Death

When a Muslim is about to die, he or she tries to say or hear the Shahadah. They were the first words that a Muslim heard at birth, and Muslims hope that they will also be the last words they hear before they die. When Muslims learn of a death, they say in sympathy, "To Allah we belong and to Him is our return."

In Islamic tradition, the family washes the body of the person who died at least three times. Men are wrapped in three pieces of cloth and women in five. While the body is carried to the grave site, the family members touch the coffin or shroud.

Muslims believe that the body should be in direct contact with the earth. The coffin is opened at the grave site, and earth is sprinkled around the head of the deceased. Muslims paint a marker on their plain coffins. The marker ensures that the head is tilted toward the Ka'bah, the holiest Muslim shrine in Mecca, Saudi Arabia. After the funeral, there is a period of mourning when friends and relatives visit the grieving family, bringing food and coming to pray.

(above) A Muslim family prays at home.

(below) A tombstone with Arabic writing overlooks the hills of Jerusalem.

Food in Israel

Each group of people in Israel has its own style of cooking, depending on where the people originally came from. The most common flavors are from the Middle East. Pungent garlic, fragrant **cumin**, and fiery peppers spice up Israeli food. Because olive trees grow easily in the country, olive oil is used in many foods. Fresh fruit and vegetables grown in the country are also a large part of every meal.

Pita

The flat bread, *pita*, is sold everywhere in Israel. People use it to scoop up Middle Eastern spreads such as *hummous*, which is mashed chick peas mixed with spices, and *tahini*, which is sesame paste. The pocket-like bread is often stuffed with lamb, eggplant, or raw vegetables for an Israeli-style sandwich.

Falafel

One of the most popular foods in Israel is *falafel*. To make a *falafel* sandwich, chickpeas and spices are ground up, molded into balls, deep-fried, and put into *pitas* with vegetables and *tahini*. You do not have to look very far to find *falafel*. Street vendors sell them everywhere!

(above) **Falafel** *sandwiches are a real hand and mouthful!*

(left) *A bread seller balances a huge basket of* **pita** *on his head.*

Meals

An Israeli breakfast is hearty and may include vegetables, olives, cheese, and sometimes even fish. For many people, lunch is the main meal of the day. They might eat a *kebob*, a special type of burger made with ground beef or lamb, or *shishlik*, meat marinated in garlic and oil, threaded onto skewers, and cooked on a barbecue. Lunch is not usually eaten until almost 3:00 p.m., after school is over for the day. Dinner is a lighter meal of salad or fish eaten after 7:00 p.m.

Keeping kosher

Many Jewish people keep *kosher*. The dietary laws of Judaism, called *kashrut*, do not allow people to eat shellfish or fish without scales, such as catfish. Pork, or pig meat, is forbidden. Livestock must be slaughtered and butchered in a specific way. Meat and dairy products are never eaten together. In fact, in *kosher* homes, there are two sets of kitchenware, one set for meat and one for dairy. Some religious homes also have two refrigerators to keep the meat separate from the dairy, and some even have two dishwashers!

Halal/Haram

Muslims also have dietary laws that they must follow. Foods that are permitted are called *halal*, which means that they are lawful: the food has been slaughtered and prepared according to the instructions of the Qur'an. For example, while slaughtering an animal, the butcher must cry out the name of Allah. Foods that are forbidden by the Qur'an, such as pork and alcohol, are called *haram*, which means that they are banned.

(above) A hillside olive grove. Olive trees are hardy and live for a long time.

(above) This colorful display in a Tel Aviv market is hard for olive lovers to resist!

(above) Spices make foods tasty. These are sold in bulk at a market.

Life on a kibbutz

When Jews started returning to Palestine, as Israel was called in the 1800s and early 1900s, much of the land was **desolate**. Farming was difficult. Many Jews did not have enough money to set up their own farms. They needed equipment to till the soil, and **irrigation** systems to water the land. So they pooled their money and set up **collective farms** called *kibbutzim*.

Cooperation

The *kibbutz* is based on cooperation and sharing. Everyone works hard so everyone can live comfortably. Except for a small monthly allowance, people who live on a *kibbutz*, called *kibbutzniks*, are not paid. All of their basic needs are met in return for the work they do for the community. The *kibbutz* provides clothes, food, health care, and education. Any profit that a *kibbutz* earns is used to buy equipment or to build new homes for the *kibbutz*. If a *kibbutz* has extra, it might build a swimming pool, a recreation center, or concert hall.

Family life

Kibbutzniks live in small apartments and houses. There is a shared dining room but in many *kibbutzim* today, families eat in their own kitchens. In the early days of the *kibbutzim*, children lived with other children in a building called the children's house rather than with their parents. It is now more common for them to live with their families.

The routine

Some adults spend the day farming, while others teach or help manage the *kibbutz*. Adults take turns doing routine jobs, such as serving food in the dining room or doing laundry. During the day, when their parents work, children spend the day at a daycare or school run by the *kibbutz*. Students are expected to work on the *kibbutz* as well. They often help with **harvest** to learn how the *kibbutz* operates.

*Teenagers add their pickings to the **kibbutz's** apple harvest.*

Moshav

Moshavim are another type of farming community in Israel. Like *kibbutzim*, they are based on cooperation. Farm machinery is shared and people work together to sell their produce. On a *moshav*, unlike on a *kibbutz*, families own their homes and farm their own land.

Ideas change

Kibbutzim are changing. Instead of relying only on farming, many *kibbutzim* have factories. In the early days of *kibbutzim*, people were not encouraged to have personal belongings. Everything was shared, sometimes even clothes. Today, many families own their appliances, and sometimes even their home. As *kibbutz* modernize, the way of life is changing. Some *kibbutzim* now charge a small fee for dining hall meals or laundry service. In many *kibbutzim*, *kibbutzniks* now earn salaries. *Kibbutzim* are regaining popularity in Israel.

*(above) Some **kibbutzim** run poultry farms, factories, wineries, or even daycare centers.*

*(right) A **kibbutznik** stirs a huge cauldron of steaming soup that will feed the entire **kibbutz**.*

For hundreds of years, Bedouin have moved from place to place through the Negev Desert. While today many are settling in permanent homes in cities such as Be'er Sheva, others still live traditional lifestyles.

Camels: The perfect desert vehicle

Camels are very important to the lifestyle of the Bedouin. They carry heavy loads over long distances in the desert. Camels can survive up to six weeks in winter without water, but in the summer they must drink every three days.

Camels' faces are specially designed for the desert. Their extra long eyelashes and nostrils that close help protect them from blowing sand.

Passenger or freight?

Female camels are strong and are preferred for riding. They can gallop at 20 kilometers/hour (12 miles/hour) and continue at a fast pace for several hours. Male camels are used as beasts of burden to carry the Bedouins' heavy luggage of tents and trading goods. If a camel thinks that a load is too heavy, it will sit down and refuse to move.

Camels provide more than transport. Their dung is used for fuel and their urine is used for shampoo. It leaves hair shiny and gets rid of lice. Look closely at a camel's hide and you will see a *wasm*, a **brand** that is the camel owner's identification.

A cup of coffee with a sheikh

Arabs have grown, prepared, and traded coffee for centuries. Thick, bitter Arab coffee is usually served to guests of the Bedouin. Coffee brewing is an involved process, and the more important the guest, the more detailed the **ritual**. A host will rarely make the coffee himself – he has a guest to tend to! A wealthy sheikh may have his most trusted servant prepare the coffee.

After a fire is lit, freshly ground and roasted coffee beans are thrown into a pot of strong coffee made the day before, and boiling water is added. The mixture is boiled again, and fragrant **cardamom** pods are thrown in the brew. Before the guest can drink the coffee, it must be poured first into one pot, then into another, and then poured through a strainer. When finished the coffee, the guest shakes the empty cup with six flicks of the wrist. The host then refills the cup and passes it on.

(above) A Bedouin grinds freshly fire-roasted coffee beans with a mortar and pestle.

(above) Tents in the desert need to be tied down tightly, so strong winds do not blow them away.

(right) A Bedouin woman spins goat wool into thread. She will weave the thread into thick fabric for a tent or thinner fabric for clothing.

When Israel signed a **peace treaty** with Egypt in 1979, it ended 30 years of hostility and war between the two countries. Since then, leaders in the Middle East have tried to find peaceful solutions to other conflicts, but the meetings are difficult and talks often break down.

Jews and Arabs spend an evening together discussing peace and stability.

Jews and Palestinians

Jews around the world celebrated when Israel became a country in 1948. However, Arabs who lived on the land before 1948 felt that their country was being taken away from them. To this day, most Palestinians feel that they have a historical right to part of Palestine. They hope to create a Palestinian state in the West Bank and Gaza Strip. Control over some of this territory has already been transferred to the Palestinians, but they are still waiting for the homeland that has been promised to them.

An Israeli school teacher writes the word peace on a blackboard. All Israelis want peace and security, but it is hard to agree on how to achieve it.

Differences of opinion

Among the Jewish population of Israel, there are many different opinions on how to achieve peace with Israel's neighbors and with the Palestinians in the West Bank and Gaza Strip. Some feel that Israel should **negotiate** with its neighbors and trade land for a guarantee of peace. Others feel that Israel should keep the land it has acquired and continue to expand Jewish settlement in the territories marked for the Palestinians.

Hope for peace

Many people in Israel and in countries around the world are working hard to solve Israel's and the Middle East's problems. There has been some progress, but the peace and security that all of Israel's residents, both Jewish and Arab, long for is still a dream. Each time violence flares up, an old or new solution is put forward. Israel is a **democratic** country, where people often debate the future of the country and the pathways to peace.

Glossary

ancestors People from whom one is descended

anti-Semitism A hatred of Jewish people

brand An identifying mark that is burned onto the hide of livestock with a hot iron

cardamom An Indian herb with aromatic seeds that are used as a spice

circumcise To remove the foreskin of a penis

collective farm A farm that is run jointly by a group of people

coming of age The time when a young person reaches adulthood

cumin A spice native to the Mediterranean and common in Middle Eastern cooking

democratic A state or area where government is elected by the people

desolate Deserted and uninhabitable

Diaspora The scattering of the Jews outside the land of Israel

discriminate To treat unfairly because of race, religion, gender, or other factors

empire A group of countries under one ruler

environment The physical conditions in which someone lives and works

famine An extreme shortage of food in a country or large area

haggle To bargain or argue back and forth over a price

harvest The gathering of crops

holy Having special religious importance

homeland A country that is identified with a particular people or ethnic group

immigrate To come to settle in a different country

irrigation The supplying of water to land using ditches, sprinklers, and other means

kippah A head covering worn by many Jews for prayer and by some religious Jews all the time

minority A small group of people within a larger group

negotiate To meet with others in order to reach a compromise or agreement

peace treaty An agreement that is signed by two or more warring countries to end hostility

prophet A person who is believed to speak on behalf of God

rabbi A Jewish religious leader

rebellion An uprising to overthrow an existing government or set of rulers

refugee A person who leaves his or her home or country because of danger

ritual A formal custom in which several steps are faithfully followed

synagogue A Jewish place of worship

traditions Customs that are handed down from one generation to another

truce An agreement that ends hostilities between two or more groups

yeshiva A Jewish day school that focuses on religious study

Index